YOU WILL SMILE AGAIN

Angela D. Johnson

outskirtspress
DENVER, COLORADO

It was Saturday evening, and I was awaiting a call from Latrice, who had gone shopping at an area mall. Latrice had gone shopping to prepare for an upcoming family vacation to Orlando. Latrice and her friend were in search of matching outfits, which they didn't find at our local mall. Her last words to me were, "I'll call you when I get there."

About three hours had gone by and still no call from Latrice. Looking back, I recall holding the telephone in anticipation of her call. I must break here and address all children, teenagers, or adult children who are living at home with your parents, or perhaps you've moved out, or even own your own home: *Let someone know where you are at all times.* I know you think you are not a baby anymore, but you will always be a child to your mother. It doesn't hurt to let them know what direction you're headed in, and who will be accompanying you. Even if you think no one cares, continue reading. You'll find out that more people care about you than you really know.

I, too, am a protective mother, so I called Latrice's cell phone; and, to my surprise, I got no answer. Now this really made me feel uneasy, so I whispered a prayer, and began watching a movie to occupy my mind. Finally the telephone rang; it was my cousin, just calling to say hi. I began talking to him. He always asked how everyone was, and since I was still a little uneasy, I told him I was awaiting a call from Latrice, who'd gone to the mall earlier and hadn't called. Latrice and I were not only mother and daughter, we were basically inseparable friends.

 I know, I know, you are not supposed to be your daughter's friend; you are supposed to be her mother. Well, I was both. I remember some of our special talks. My husband and son would be downstairs watching sports, and she'd come and lay across my bed and we'd share our day. Latrice was especially excited about our upcoming vacation; she was busy trying to figure out what we'd do while on vacation. She was the type of person that wanted to know the what, when, and where about everything. We'd always keep each other informed, but this day was different.

As I continued my telephone conversation with my cousin, the door bell rang. At the door were two police officers coming to tell us the horrific news.

One officer said, "Your daughter was involved in a terrible accident."

At that point, my whole body went numb. A rush of questions followed, and then the unbelievable truth, she didn't survive. I guess, I wasn't listening closely enough or didn't understand.

I looked at my husband, and said, "Okay, let's go to the hospital."

My husband looked helplessly back at me and said, "Angie, she's gone."

I totally lost it; I fell to the floor, grabbed my husband's leg and screamed continuously for the next half hour.

It is almost impossible to explain. It's a feeling I wouldn't wish on anyone. I realize that on our planet many have and will continue to experience this type of loss each and every day. They will die, whether by natural means, accident, or at the hands of others. BUT IT HURTS. And I'm writing to let you know, with the help of God, you can get through this.

Romans 8:18
For I reckon that the sufferings of this present time are not worthy to be compared with the glory which shall be revealed in us.

I recall as a child growing up, after attending a church mother's funeral, I prayed and asked God to let me be the first to die in my family. Silly, you might say, but even though I was a child, I remember feeling the pain of her family members. I never wanted to experience the full effect of what I felt that day. But, in December, 1996, my father, the late Bishop King E. Burnett, made his final journey to his heavenly home. It, too, was hard; it didn't seem real. What I saw so many go through was now falling upon me. I wasn't a child anymore; I was married and had children. Remembering how I felt then, I realized they too must endure this loss. I remember after Latrice found out her grandfather was gone, she clung to me. We talked about it; and I assured Latrice that her Pop-Pop didn't just die, he went to heaven. Latrice would later write a poem about the loss of her Pop-Pop.

A couple of years later, my mother-in-law, Mother Sarah Johnson, went home to be with the Lord. This also was very upsetting to Latrice. We again talked about heaven; Grandmom was no longer in pain. Grandmom was safely resting in the arms of her maker.

Philippians 1:21
For me to live is Christ, and to die is gain.

I am forever grateful that I was taught that life does not end at death. One day we all will have to meet our maker. It is of utmost importance to live each day ready to meet your maker. If you never knew or believed in God, let me tell you, He is real and He is soon to return.

I remember, in the middle of the screams, asking God to please guard my mind. You see, I'm a born again believer. I'd been raised in the church my whole life, and I was always taught that there was a mighty God who loved and cared about me, and His name was Jesus.

Isaiah 26:3
Thou wilt keep him in perfect peace, whose mind is stayed on thee: because he trusteth in thee.

My father was a pastor, my father-in-law pastored. I knew about my triune God, and believed in the power of His might. But this experience would make me to know my God in a more intimate way.

While I was screaming and holding on for dear life to my husband's leg, he alerted our families of the horrific news. Within an hour, my house was packed with family and friends. I remember the first family member to arrive, my wonderful sister-in-law, Barbara, grabbing me as we sorely wept together. Latrice was also like a daughter to Barbara and Thomas, who had no daughters of their own. The next few hours I remember going from arm to arm as family members tried to console me.

In came our brothers, and sisters, aunts, and uncles, nieces, nephews, and cousins. They all came to offer support, to help each other get through this. It sounds unbelievable in today's society; it seems as though those types of families don't exist anymore. But I give God praise for blessing me with loving and caring family members.

In came my son's friends, one by one, showing their concern and support. I believe even some of my dedicated church family came bringing prayers of comfort.

It is a true saying that bad news travels fast. I heard the story was even headlining the eleven o'clock news: Local high school senior killed in a horrible car accident. I understand the local news has to be reported, but shouldn't they be more sensitive to the families involved? What if you were in that family's predicament, would you want to hear it on the news?

I remember the telephones ringing non-stop: distant family and friends, calling in disbelief, wanting to verify the information. Visitors poured in, looking around at the masses of people, in search of myself, my husband, and my son.

You see, both my husband and I have rather large families. My husband is one of twelve siblings, and I am one of six siblings. Each of our parents also had ten plus siblings, most of whom live in the surrounding area. So imagine family plus friends in a rancher.

All of a sudden, I glimpsed my sister, Karen, and her family, coming through the doorway. I got up, and went to the door to help her with her four kids. Okay, I know what you're thinking, *Wait, you went to help Karen and her four kids?* Remember, I prayed and asked God to keep my mind. Well, it was at this point I knew he had. For it was at this point God let me know that I wasn't the only one experiencing unexplainable pain. There were others like Latrice's many aunts and uncles who watched her grow up and cherished her company, Latrice's two younger cousins, Ciera and Taylor, who Latrice would often babysit, and their parents Ish and Cheryl; we were always together. Latrice's male and female cousins who thought of Latrice as their sister or the cousin they just loved being around. A lot of people cared for Latrice, and they, too, were having a hard time dealing with the loss. I'm sure there are people who care about you too.

Karen and I are very close; we were actually born a year apart. You could say we were uniquely close, for we married brothers. Anyway, because we married brothers, we were together quite often, and our children were close. Especially close was my niece, Lauren, who was truly one of Latrice's favorite cousins.

Karen was coming through the doorway with Lauren and Karen literally hanging on her; while Lawrence and Karl desperately held on to her coat. I grabbed Lauren and, by the power of God through me, began to console her. I know I didn't have any strength at this point, so it had to be the power of God that settled me down enough to console someone else.

Galatians 6:2
Bear ye one another's burdens, and so fulfill the law of Christ.

How is it possible to feel someone else's hurt while you yourself are hurting? It is only through the power of God. Yes, Latrice was my daughter, but she was also my husband's daughter, my son's sister and, at that particular moment, Lauren's favorite cousin. Here is an  amazing point: while consoling Lauren, I felt consolation. I can only tell you how I felt.

It seemed as if all eyes were on me. What was I going to do next? Was I okay? In walked Latrice's favorite teacher, who heard and actually caught a cab to my house to see if it was true. Once again, I got up and went over to console her, feeling consolation in her embrace.

I would like to make a small request of those who wish to show concern to someone who has just lost a family member. Please be polite, don't ask a lot of questions, just embrace them and say a quiet prayer for them. It is difficult for the grieving family to contain their own thoughts. Any questions or details at that point are unimportant. Please remember they are grieving, be polite, and pray for that individual or family. They need God to help them through this.

I guess it was around twelve midnight before my loving family began to leave. Just as they had arrived, carload by carload, the house began to empty. Finally, it was just me, my husband, and my son, sitting together, trying to console each other. It was literally one of the longest nights of my life. My poor husband and son took turns dozing, trying to keep an ever-so-watchful eye on me. I know we all needed and wanted so desperately to go to sleep and wake up as if from a bad dream. I dozed off, and was awakened to realize this wasn't a dream. It was real. My Latrice, our Latrice was gone. We'd never see her again. I began wailing, that feeling of my heart being ripped from my chest returned.

Even as I write, the tears flow, but its okay. I'm determined to help someone. Even if you have experienced or may be experiencing a sudden loss, I am here to tell you, with God's help, you will smile again!

The Lord has blessed us to make it through the night. I went to use the restroom, and had a meltdown. My husband came rushing in to console me. While consoling me, I saw his tears begin to roll. This was hard, but I didn't want to overwhelm my husband, for he was hurting just as much as I. Lord, help us. The telephone rang. It was my sister, Karen, who told me to get dressed and put on a nice pant suit.

Karen knew the grueling day that was now ahead of us. My sister, Karen, is a pastor--I should say, my pastor. She and her husband became our Joshua and Caleb after my dad's exit to glory. So she knew quite well what the next few days would entail. Yes, funeral arrangements.

I avoided television for fear of hearing or seeing clips of the accident. But, of course, the local newspaper picked up the story and ran articles the entire week. One day they even called my house for an interview. Again I ask, please be considerate to family members facing such a crisis. My family members brought some of the articles over, which I kept as a keepsake. One article mentioned that almost half of the high school population did not show up for school one day, so they dismissed early. I told you more people care about you than you think.

As we began getting dressed, the phone rang again; it was my little sister, Janet. Janet always reminds me that I'm only a couple of years older than she. Latrice was also very close to her Aunt Janet and Uncle Matt, who took her passing very hard. Latrice's first job was actually being Janet's shampoo girl. Janet was calling to see how we were doing, and I told her that I was trying to get dressed but my phones were ringing unceasingly. Not to worry, she was on her way. My two sisters-in-law, Barbara and Juanita, called. They were on their way. We would have the constant support of family for the next eight days.

With our family's non-stop support came a lot of food. Yes, we have soul food chefs in our families. In particular, I remember my cousin, Patty, who also has a special connection to me and my husband. While we were dating, Patty was our cheerleader. You see, we were only fifteen years old and madly in love. So many said at that time, we didn't know what real love was, but thirty-three years later, we are happily married and gracefully growing old together.

Patty has also been blessed with the awesome gift of helping. Patty, my cousin Vanessa, and a few others, love supporting families in their time of need. "Well, Angie," Patty said, "my group wants to cook for you. What would you like to eat?" But at this point I didn't really feel like eating, so she came up with a little thanksgiving meal.

It looked, smelled, and tasted good, and after her persistence, I managed to eat about a third of the food on my plate.

Eating is usually not one of your strong points while you are grieving. You are having a hard time thinking. Eating just doesn't seem that important. It seems as though your taste buds are gone. The food smells and looks good, but you don't really have an appetite. Take it from me: listen to your family members. You need food to help keep your strength up. Please eat; even if it's just a half of sandwich or a cup of soup, you have to eat.

Not only did we have the support of my family, our friends played an amazing part in those next eight days. My son's friends came to show their concern and support. There were also some of my daughter's friends who popped in. I believe one day half of the high school's baseball team came over after a game to show their support.

What? Did you say half of the high school's baseball team? Yes, you see Latrice was a senior in high school, preparing for graduation. She knew a lot of people, and was well liked by many. Latrice really couldn't help it. Not to sound biased, but she really was a beautiful young lady, with a lovable attitude. To know Latrice was to love Latrice.

It took me back. Just a few weeks before, we were assisting Latrice as she got dressed for her senior prom. I remember shopping forever for the perfect gown. We kind of procrastinated just a little. I ended up, the day before the prom, trying on dresses for Latrice at a bridal store, because she had to work. I remember my sister, Janet, and niece, Christina, making sure her makeup and hair was perfect. Latrice was beautiful!

There was my Godmother Carolyn, and my special Aunt Dorothy; who were always there for me and my family.

There were our close friends, like the Comers, Jacobs, and the McCoys, who came and offered support every step of the way. They were reminiscing about old times, sharing funny stories, offering extra shoulders to lean on.

There was Ms. Lillie, who had also lost her daughter a couple of years prior. She was one of the people I immediately wanted to talk to. Ms. Lillie would be one of the people who would help assist me through this grueling process. I'm not saying I

didn't want to talk to people, but at this time I didn't want to try to explain how I felt. I especially wanted to talk to people who had experienced what I was now experiencing.

There were my awesome, loving, caring, co-workers. From upper management, middle management, to regular workers, ex-co-workers: some called, some sent cards, some sent flowers and some even bought food. I remember some, (I don't want to leave anyone's name out) even came to visit me. I wasn't home at the time, but they showed their love to my family members that were home.

We decided that Latrice would wear her graduation gown in her casket. Her Aunt Mary willingly went to the school to pick it up for us. That took care of one piece of her clothing; she still needed something under the gown. So, my sisters quickly whisked me off in search of an outfit. Our sisters were so supportive.

Yes, even to this day, I've even been blessed to have caring co-workers. When my children were younger, Lynda would make sure that every holiday they had a nice tasty treat. Lynda and Victoria both loved talking to Latrice when she would call me at work. Then there are others, whom I will mention later, who helped me in my quiet times.

There were also neighbors who showed their support. I remember coming home one day from making the funeral service arrangements. Our neighbor across the street flagged my husband down. He said, "I have something for you." Out he came with about six flower arrangements that he had so graciously held for us from the delivery man. Yes, you are right; I was also blessed with pretty nice neighbors.

There was our local high school, and School Board, who called, came, and asked what they could do. As we continued making the service arrangements, their help and support would prove to be genuine.

There was prayer and support from different churches with whom we fellowship, who proved to offer surpassing kindness.

We continued on with the service arrangements; there were calls from many wanting to assist. My sister, Karen, worked diligently, ensuring that this would be a home going service, not a funeral. In other words, she knew this would be hard for all of us, so she wanted everything upbeat. She wanted the music blaring and the choir/songstress, anointed.

Janet relentlessly kept track of flowers, cards, phone calls with an ever-so-careful eye on me. Matt willingly saw to it that there were drinks and ice, necessities, and trash duty. Barbara was constantly trying to store all the food that kept pouring in. Juanita kept an ever-so-careful eye on my husband. My nephews kept an ever-so-careful eye on my son.

Now, you ask, how was I feeling at this point? Well, the days passed quickly, but the nights were sad and slow. Somehow, I was sort of okay while the house was full of people. They came in crying and I was consoling them. At night, it was just us: me, my husband, and my son... no Latrice. I walked past her room, and the bed was empty. It got so bad I had to close her door, so I wouldn't look for her. I wondered how my husband and son were feeling? I knew they were hurting, but were they feeling they had to be strong for me? I was even blaming myself for allowing Latrice to go to the mall. It was hard!

As the service date drew closer, my out-of-town family members began to arrive. They came by car, by airplane, by van, by bus. They all came. Young and old, my family, my husband's family, our close friends---more shoulders to lean on, more happy reminiscing, my family support was here.

I remember my nephew, Milton, sitting on the couch, talking on his walkie talkie telephone. It immediately reminded me of the police officers' radios that kept going off the night we were informed of Latrice's passing. Did Milton know? No, he had no idea, but he quickly turned it off and gave me a big hug. Milton was hurting too. He'd lived with us for about nine months, and was like a big brother to Latrice. And as they grew older, she'd even try to give Milton pointers on the proper way to dress for a date.

Seven days quickly came and went. The days were busy and full, the nights stretched out forever. But by the strength of God and the prayers of the righteous, we kept going. You see, at this point, we really couldn't pray for ourselves. We couldn't do our normal family prayer before we went to bed;

we were missing someone in our prayer circle. Latrice was gone. *Lord, help us.*

It was now the dreadful day of the viewing. We arrived at the funeral home and saw family members were in place. The funeral home was very small and could not begin to contain our families, so I knew the others that were not present were undoubtedly praying. I knew people were praying for us, because we would not have made it through the past seven days without God's help.

James 5:16
The effectual fervent prayer of a righteous man availeth much.

There were times when I was alone, usually when I was in the bathroom, I'd have a meltdown. My meltdowns were so severe; at times I'd almost end up on the floor. I would try and smother my wailing with my towel. I didn't want to call out and upset my husband or my son. I thought back on what I'd heard preached across the pulpit so many times.

I then whispered, "Lord, help me." Immediately a peace would come over me. An unbelievable calm came over me. My crying stopped, yes, it stopped. I looked up and said, *Thank you, Jesus. My God is awesome!*

Psalms 8:26
Likewise the Spirit also helpeth our infirmities: for we know not what we should pray for as we ought: but the Spirit itself maketh intercession for us with groanings which cannot be uttered

I cannot imagine going through without God. Maybe you are reading this book and you may be thinking, *Wow, God did that for you? Will He help me?* Yes, just ask.

We walked into the funeral parlor and our families were all surrounding the casket and weeping. They began to step back, and I glimpsed a beautiful pink casket which was holding my daughter's body. The last time I'd seen Latrice she was on her way to the mall.

As you can imagine, I was shaking and crying. Never, ever, had I imagined seeing my daughter in a casket. She was only eighteen, she hadn't graduated, and she was just about to begin her adult life. Why did this happen to my daughter?

I had my two crutches (my husband and son) by my side and we headed toward the casket. We continued toward the casket, and they had chairs waiting to seat me. I remember thinking, *Wow, this is real. They said Latrice was gone, but now I'm sitting in front of the evidence. I know I picked the flowers and the casket; the service arrangements are in place. But this is all I have left of my daughter. She's lying here in a casket. She's not smiling or laughing or even talking, she's really gone. God, please help me.*

I cry for a while, and begin to again feel God's presence overtake me with calm. It was like He was saying, *"It's okay, Angie, she's with me. You will see her again, but right now she's with me."* Thank you, Jesus.

There Latrice lay, dressed in her graduation gown. My sisters and nieces began straightening her gown and I noticed that Latrice's bangs had been cut. What? You must understand that everyone knew how Latrice felt about her hair. Latrice had long beautiful hair; Janet was the only one who trimmed her hair. But it was all good; it helped break up some of the tension in the air.

After the viewing I went over to my sister, Karen's, house to greet some of my family members who had come in from

Florida. Lots of food, hugs, smiles, and reminiscing followed. I received a reassuring hug from my cousin, Janie Mae, who had lost her son a couple of years earlier. Wow, I was exhausted and must get rest; tomorrow would be here before I knew it.

Tomorrow arrived; we awakened, made sure everyone ate something and we got dressed. Additional families from Virginia had arrived to greet and support us. It was time, the limo now arrived. We headed to our church to meet with the hundreds of other family members and make the dreaded ride to the hosting church.

We arrived at our church and disembarked from the limo to have special prayer. Wow, our church parking lot was full of family, and they were all here to support us and each other. More hugs, and then the prayer began. I refused to close my eyes; I didn't want to start crying. But the tears began to roll. *God help me, help my family. Thank you, Jesus.*

The prayer ended, and we all loaded up to go to the host church. As we were leaving, I turned to look and there must have been at least fifty cars behind us.

We tried to get the biggest church in the area, since we knew we had a lot of family members. Thankfully the host church pastor graciously and willingly allowed us the use of his church. We turned the corner and all I could see was people and cars, everywhere. The limo pulled into the parking lot, I noticed the parking attendants who were flagging us in were our local high school security guards. This was totally surreal.

Our families lined up to go into the church. *Wow, we really do have a lot of family.* We heard the music blaring; we began to enter the church. All I remember is walking in the church door, the music blaring and I recall safely arriving at my seat. By that I mean, I didn't try to look around as I entered the church; I was taking each minute as it came.

After reaching my seat, my mind ran through all the hundreds of family members who had come from both far and near, and I wanted to make sure they were seated. I began looking around; the church was packed to the maximum. I was only able to hope we were all seated.

The moderator was Bishop William Young Jr., a very close family friend who thought of Latrice as a niece. Bishop Young began the service, alerting everyone that this would be a homegoing service and not a funeral, which held to be true.

From the beautiful programs, to the opening prayer, to the awesome psalmist, to the powerful praise dancers (who were all Latrice's cousins); to the touching words of encouragement, to the stirring eulogy by my sister, Karen, Latrice's homegoing was truly beautiful. I remember a couple of times during the service, a roll call was made, and Latrice's name was called out; the entire church filled up with a roar. But now we came to the final viewing. *This is a place where even the strongest person struggles. Lord, please help us.*

I saw students with specially made t-shirts, I saw teachers, I saw friends, I saw co-workers, I saw family members, and then I began falling apart. It was almost my turn, I began thinking, *I can't do this. This is too much, I can't do this. Lord, help me.* My husband and son helped me up and here I go. I became weak and could hardly stand, Lord, help me. Then a still small voice whispered, *Angie, you don't have long, you must say goodbye.* I lifted my head up and began stroking Latrice's hair, I kissed her goodbye and we covered her face with the lace cloth and closed the casket. Lord, help us.

I again heard the music blaring; the army of ushers began taking out the beautiful flower arrangements, the beautiful pink casket was rolled out, the clergymen followed, and now we too joined the recession. It was over, Lord help us.

We now headed to the burial ground which was in the adjourning city. Our limo and tons of cars now exited the parking lot. We were then, graciously and safely, led out of the city limits by our local police department. Arriving at the burial ground, we exited the limo, and awaited the many family members coming to join us.

I was kind of numb, and just following along. I felt somewhat at ease that Latrice's grave was right next to her Pop-Pop's (Bishop King Burnett). *Okay, I can do this, help me Lord.* The graveside service was held, and it was time to return to our church for the wake.

Back at the church, the smell of good food hit us as we got out of the car. Inside, the hall was packed, more hugs and kisses. *It's over, help us, Lord.* I nibbled on a little food, and began chatting with family and friends. Hours passed, people started to leave, we thanked them for coming, and we thanked everyone for helping. *What now? It's over, Lord, help us.*

We headed home, and a couple of family members joined us. More reminiscing, old stories, especially the story about when I accompanied Latrice's on her first date. Yes, I did, we went to the movies; they sat up high and I sat so I could clearly see them.

After the movies, the young man was informed of how special Latrice was. I told him Latrice wasn't like other girls he may have dated, Latrice was not to be treated as other girls, and she was special. Was my message strong? Yes. Did he receive my message? Yes. How do I know? He came back again

That night, the house was really, really quiet. It was a lot…. different, it was just us. Wow, that was different. I mean, for the last eight days, it had been non-stop people, non-stop phone calls, non-stop noise, *Lord, help us.*

The next day was Sunday, and as always, we attended the eleven a.m. service. We had some family members who would be leaving to go back South during the service. One in particular was my cousin, Tina. As the service was going on, Tina was right there by my side. Then came the point where my departing family members began to leave and they were trying to get Tina's attention. I said, *"Okay Tina, you have to go."*

Tina grabbed me and would not let me go. I told her it was alright; she still wouldn't let go and kept telling me she loved me, and didn't want to leave me.

I said, *"I know Tina, but you have to go, I will be alright."* She continued to hold on to me. I actually had to ask her boyfriend's assistance to pull her away. You might say that's weird. Well, listen to this, a couple of years later, Tina would also lose a child.

Is it premonition or is it the Lord's way of letting you know you, too, will experience a similar plight. I remember on a few occasions, prior to my Latrice's passing, feeling extremely uneasy. One day I was at work and we were all called to a meeting. We were told about a co-worker who had lost her son. He had drowned. There was another day when I was reading my Daily Bread, and there was a story of a man who had lost his teenage daughter in a car accident. For some strange reason I kept that Daily Bread. Finally there was Ms. L. daughter, who was my co-worker. Someone took her life. This one hit me hard. I was really upset, and cried uncontrollably at her homegoing service.

That Sunday after church, we would also have a few out-of-town friends who followed us home. It was the Willis family who we also considered our family. My sisters and their families also joined us. It was a very nice visit. We thanked them for coming, and everyone slowly departed. *Lord, help us.*

The next morning was different. The phones were no longer ringing, the house was quiet, no one was moving around. We didn't have any pending plans. *What now? Lord, help us.*

I got up and went downstairs to the basement. The Lord reminded me of the videos my cousin Jay had given me. Thank you, Jay, for listening to the voice of the Lord. I grabbed those videos and began watching them. When I got done watching the second video, the phone rang. It was my sister, Janet, just checking on us. I'm okay," I said, "I was watching some preaching videos."

A couple of hours later, I got a call from my sister, Karen, just checking on us. "I'm okay," I said. "I was watching some preaching videos." Then my sister-in-law, Juanita, called to check on us.

She continued talking to my husband for a while. I'd just lie down on the couch, and watch the videos for the next couple of hours. My husband called down to me, "You want to go get something to eat," he asked.

I replied, "No, I'm not hungry.

He said, "Honey, we have to eat."

That became my daily pattern. I didn't want to go anywhere. I still didn't really have an appetite; I only ate to appease my family. I didn't want to talk. I began to slowly slip into depression. Things just weren't the same. I was in a lot of pain; I missed my daughter.

I began blaming myself, *I should have kept Latrice home that day. Maybe I should have gone with them. Maybe it's my fault. What is my husband and my son thinking, are they blaming me too?* It was hard. *Lord, please help me.*

My husband and I truly love each other, but this placed a strain on our relationship. I guess we both were feeling the same way. It was painful, it was hard to eat, hard to talk, hard to think. And don't even think about smiling. *What in the world is there to smile about? Our baby is gone. Lord, help us.*

You may be reading this book and you ask, *"Why do you keep asking the Lord to help you? You are not alone, you have your husband, you have your son, and you have your family members. Can't you talk to them, ask them? You might be thinking you were left with no one.*

I would respond and say yes, and they helped. But they could do nothing for my hurting heart. The only one I  know that can reach in and heal a hurting heart is the Lord; for only God can heal the heart.

Psalms 116:1-4
I love the LORD, because he hath heard my voice and my supplications. Because he hath inclined his ear unto me, therefore will I call upon him as long as I live. The sorrows of death compassed me, and the pains of hell gat hold upon me: I found trouble and sorrow. Then called I upon the name of the LORD; O LORD, I beseech thee, deliver my soul.

The pain was unbelievable, my whole body was hurting.

Was this okay, was this normal? I had to go to the doctors so that I wouldn't get fired from my job. They prescribed medicine that would only make me feel worse. Lord, help me.

One day my son brought me the mail. I saw what looked like a card. I noticed it was from Vickie, I thought awww.., I opened the card, and it was a picture of an adorable puppy and it said *Thinking of you.* And, of course, I cried. A couple of days later, I got a card from Deanna, with beautiful flowers, which said *I'm praying for you.* About a week later, I got a card from Nancy, it read, *My thoughts are with you.* Vickie and Deanna would continue sending me cards on every important holiday for the next two years.

I even remember one week my payroll buddies, along with Ms. Lillie, insisted we do lunch. The payroll buddies included Christy, Deanna, Brenda, Sherry, Wendy, and Theresa. They all wanted to see me, to make sure I was okay.

I didn't want to go but they were very persistent, so I went. I still had no appetite, and ended up taking most of my food home. It was as if I was afraid to go around people, afraid they'd ask me questions.

The Lord also laid us upon the hearts of my two special cousins, Lucrecia and Samere. They would also begin to call and check on us. They were also adamant about bringing gifts on special holidays. You see, I basically celebrate every holiday. My children always received little gifts even on Valentine's Day. God had begun to use special people to bless me. They were not doing it to be seen, God just placed us on their hearts. In addition to the small gifts and timely telephone call's, Lucrecia and Samere always came with beautiful smiles.

God had placed me on someone's mind, and they responded with those cards, those timely phone calls. These gestures meant a lot. Has God ever laid someone on your mind? Pray for them, call them, send them a card. God placed them on your mind for a reason. It's as if God is requesting you to physically reach out and touch someone.

My cousin, Latosha, stopped me one day at church and said, "We need to have lunch together." I remembered the adorable silly photo she and Latrice took together while at a sleep over. Latrice had the photo hanging from her bedroom door. How sweet that Latosha sensed the void that I was experiencing.

I'd experience my first Mothers Day without my daughter. Lord, help me. I woke up that morning very sensitive, of course. I began to get text messages from Janet, Cheryl, my brothers, John and King, Lauren, and Latosha. Lord, please help me.

I went downstairs and saw the flowers and cards my husband and son had bought me which, of course, made me cry. I decided to wear a big hat to church so that it would hide my eyes. I just knew I'd cry the entire service, especially when it came time to give out cards to all mothers. We got to church and I sat between Janet and Lauren. Being sensitive, my sister, Pastor Karen, told everyone to give out cards during the offering. I had my head down and all of a sudden, I saw my precious Kayla handing me a card. Kayla and Karen have always been special to us. Kayla has not missed a Mother's day since then. My nieces, Ciera and Taylor, gave me a card. My nieces, Deja and Saviah, gave me a card. *Lord, this is hard, please help me.*

The Lord told me to concentrate on the true meaning of the holiday. *Okay Lord, its Mother's Day, I'll call my mom.* I did and it made me feel better. Okay, it's Mother's Day. Thank you, Lord, for my mother.

Weeks went by before we realized it was a couple of days before Latrice's class graduation. I asked my husband to take me out of town. I didn't want to hear horns or see anyone in a cap and gown. I wanted to get as far from the graduation crowd as I could. We went to Baltimore, and one night, while out to dinner, lo and behold, in walked a couple of kids in their caps and gowns celebrating with their family. This was hard. Lord, help me.

Jeremiah 29:11-12

For I know the thoughts that I think toward you, saith the LORD, thoughts of peace, and not of evil, to give you an expected end. Then shall ye call upon me, and ye shall go and pray unto me, and I will hearken unto you.

At one point, I remembered it was only a couple of weeks before that we cheered as Latrice graduated from Vocational School, along with the honor of being inducted into the Vocational Honor Society. Of course I was pretty loud when they called Latrice's name. We were so proud of her.

The next day we returned home and learned we missed an awesome graduation. The class president, who was also one of Latrice's close friends, got choked up a few times during her speech and needed assistance to finish. There were also several touching pictures in the local newspaper from the graduation.

Lord, help me.

A couple of months went by and it was my birthday. Again, I didn't want to be in town on my birthday. Away we went to Baltimore. We'd go see a movie and then go shopping. My husband was trying to help me; he knew how much I loved shopping, but not anymore. While waiting on the movie, I tried to shop. Nice mall, but it wasn't fun anymore. All of a sudden I received a couple of text messages. My sisters and niece, Christiana, were wishing me a happy birthday. I continued trying to shop, and my phone rang. It was my niece, Juanita. She wanted to wish me a happy birthday; how sweet. The Lord was using others to help me.

Months went by. One day I got a call from Ms Lillie, who, like my sisters and sister-in-law, continued to just check on us. Ms. L said, "And how are you?"

I replied, "I'm okay I guess."

She said, "I know how you are feeling."

I told her my job was bugging me because they said I should really be ready to come back to work. I had surpassed their guidelines for being away from work. She said, "Everyone is different, Angie. Everyone handles things differently. Some people go back to work immediately to keep themselves occupied."

Well, work was the last place I wanted to be; I just wasn't ready yet. She calmly said, "You are fine, that's normal."

I needed to hear that from someone who had experienced the loss of a child. This told me that what I was feeling was normal. I've learned that as you go through the loss of a loved one, you will go through stages. *Thank you, Lord!*

That next week I received a call from Lisa. Her husband and our dear friend, Dumpy, had passed away. We immediately rushed to Lisa's side. They were a beautiful couple with two wonderful children. We used to sing together in Karen's group, called *Chosen*. We used to rehearse at Karen's house, while the kids, then very small, would play on the steps. He was the best bass player in the country, not to mention his voice. I also remembered Dumpy was a key part of the band for Latrice's homegoing. The band was performing directly in front of us, and I recall him literally wiping tears during the entire service. Dumpy just loved people; he loved helping people. Now he, too, was gone. I tried to be there for Lisa and the kids just as everyone was there for me. I remember the day of Dumpy's homegoing service I learned that Tina, Dumpy's sister, had also passed that morning. I remember seeing Dumpy and Tina's mom dance the entire service. Wow, she lost two children, and she's dancing. Lord, help her. I sat in the back of the church; I couldn't dare look into another casket. It was too soon. Lord, help Lisa, the kids, his mom, and the rest of the family.

Psalms 63:3
Because thy loving kindness is better than life, my lips shall praise thee.

Thanksgiving came. Oh Lord help me. Latrice used to help me cook for Thanksgiving. She'd assist with the candied yams and the macaroni and cheese. Lord, help me. The Lord told me to try and concentrate on the real meaning of Thanksgiving. Yes, families share a scrumptious meal, but remember to give thanks. *But Lord, I'm hurting…* Remember to give thanks.

I was reminded of the homeless and the less fortunate. I was reminded of the comfort that I'd received during my worst times. I was reminded of a loving and merciful God, who I knew, and many others have only heard about. I was reminded that He was keeping and carrying us. I must give thanks on Thanksgiving, Thank you, Jesus.

It had now been eight months since Latrice's homegoing and my Pru buddies, wanted to go to dinner. They, too, were very persistent. The Pru buddies included Lynda, Vicky, Lisa, Nancy, Vickie, Brenda, Deanna, Jolee, Carol Lee, and Tammy. I know they, too, were genuinely concerned. I still was afraid of possible questions. But they were true friends; no personal questions were asked. Again I ended up taking most of my food home. After the dinner, they also insisted on giving me a twenty-year anniversary gift from the office. Wow, my mind was so full; I had forgotten about that. Lord, help me.

Christmas came. I hesitated and procrastinated about even putting a Christmas tree up. You see, Christmas was always one of my favorite holidays. I loved decorating, and I had two Christmas trees. Latrice always helped. I would decorate the upstairs tree, and Latrice would be in charge of the basement tree. In 2003, for some strange reason, I took pictures of Latrice decorating the tree. Lord, help me. Again the Lord told me, *Angie concentrate on the real meaning of Christmas.* I thought *oh my goodness, Lord, it's your birthday, you were born to die just for me. Thank you, Lord.*

A couple of weeks later, we were at our Sunday morning service and our friend, Bishop William Young, was to bring the message. After his message, he began speaking a word of life into me. He told me that what I went through was not about me. God was going to use that to help someone else.

He told me that God was going to even birth a book out of my experience. Lord, you are good!

I considered returning to work, but I needed an incentive. We were now down one vehicle, so as an incentive, I'd get a new car. We sent away for tags and since the car was my incentive, I needed special license plates. Let's see, something with my daughter's name on it. I sent in several suggestions. Thank you, Jesus! My tags contained a message that I believe came straight from God.

In the next few months, my life began to change. I began praying more, I began talking more, I began to smile again. I received a call from Lisa, who was calling to let me know that my friend, Nancy, was asking about me. Her only son had taken ill, and she wanted to talk to me. At the time I had been considering a return to work, but this call made it definite. I had to get back to work. Lisa decided to return with me. We agreed that we'd be each other's support system.

The first day back to work, I was a little hesitant. My co-workers were pre-warned not to ask me a lot of questions. They'd just hug me and tell me how happy they were to see me. I went to my desk, which, by request, was picture free. I saw Lisa come in. *We are okay. Thank you, Jesus!*

I saw Nancy, who gave me a big hug and said, "Angie, I missed you."

She began to tell me about her son's illness, and asked me to pray. Nancy was one of my co-workers who was there for me. Lord, help Nancy and her family.

It was now a couple of weeks later and I was good. I was working, and, you know, silly things always happen. I began laughing again. I was walking down the hall one day and a co-worker approached me. We spoke, and then with tears in her eyes, she asked, "How did you do it?"

This particular co-worker had lost her granddaughter.

I replied, "It was all God." I told her it was hard, but God helped me through it. Whenever I called on Him, He answered. He helped me. So, I said, "Just pray to Him, and He'll help you, too."

I returned to my desk and this humongous smile appeared on my face. I whispered, *"Thank you, God, you are awesome. I am smiling again!"*

A couple of years later Nancy's only son worsened. I told her that she should begin to cherish each day she had with her son. About a year later, her only son would pass. I took a day off to get some blood work, and I ran into Nancy. We saw each other and quickly gave each other a hug. It was that common bond of our experience. Nancy had questions like I had experienced, questions about how I used to feel. God gave me reassuring words to speak into her life. I again reminded her of the power of prayer. Lord, you are good.

It's now going on eight years since my daughter's exit to glory. God has brought many, many people into our lives. I have a wonderful husband, and a loving son, Thank you, Jesus! I have awesome family members, Thank you, Jesus! I have beautiful young ladies and coaches who encourage me every Wednesday. Thank you, Jesus! But most importantly, I have an awesome, loving, heavenly father, who sits high and looks low. He wanted me to let you know: *Hold on, I'm with you, you will smile again!*

CPSIA information can be obtained at www.ICGtesting.com
Printed in the USA
BVOW011758120412

287562BV00005B/46/P